D0251324

The

SWEETNESS

of

LIFE

The
SWEETNESS
of
LIFE

o o o

FRANÇOISE
HÉRITIER

o o o

Translated from the French
by Anthea Bell

HARPER

www.harpercollins.com

HarperCollins books may be purchased for educational, business, or sales promotional use. For information, please e-mail the Special Markets Department at SPsales@harpercollins.com.

Originally published in French as *La sel de la vie* by Odile Jacob in 2012.

English translation first published in Great Britain in 2013 by Particular Books, an imprint of Penguin Books.

FIRST U.S. EDITION PUBLISHED 2013

Designed by Leah Carlson-Stanisic

Library of Congress Cataloging-in-Publication Data has been applied for.

ISBN 978-0-06-229104-2

13 14 15 16 17   OFF/RRD   10 9 8 7 6 5 4 3 2 1

Introduction

The following text will surprise those who know me from my anthropological writings. In all humility, I claim that this is another of them: a "fantasy" born of my pen and inspiration—and it has a story behind it. One fine summer's day, if I may be allowed that expression, since the weather was appalling, I had a postcard from Scotland. A very dear friend, Professor Jean-Charles Piette, or "Monsieur Piette" as I privately think of him, was sending me a few words from the Isle of Skye. They began: "A 'stolen' week's holiday in Scotland."

I must explain that this great clinical scientist, professor of internal medicine at the Hôpital de La Pitié and greatly loved by his patients, of whom I have been one for thirty years, lives only for them and his work. I have never known him not to be on the verge of physical and mental exhaustion, devoting hours to each patient, a doctor who is capable of accompanying the day's last patient home if he or she has been kept wait-ing too long, or of going to meet another patient's train (as he once did for me), who is capable of mad generosity and equally mad whims. And here he was, talking about a "stolen" week. It leapt to the eye. Who was stealing what? Was he stealing a little respite from a world to which he owed all he could do, or was he not, instead, let-ting his all-consuming circle of acquaintances, his obsession with his work, his many and over-whelming responsibilities, deprive him of his life? *We* are stealing his life from him, I thought, he is stealing his own life from himself.

So I began replying to him along these lines: every day you are missing out on what goes into making up the sweetness of life. And what does it do for you, apart from making you feel guilty for never doing enough? I began by setting down some major trails to follow, and soon entered into the spirit of the thing, seriously wondering what is, has been, and will, I am sure, continue to be the sweetness of my own life.

So what follows here is an enumeration, an or-dinary list in one long sentence, of ideas that came to me of their own accord by fits and starts, like a long, whispered monologue. It is about sensations, perceptions, emotions, minor pleasures and major joys, sometimes profound disillusionment and even pain, although my mind dwells more readily on the luminous than on the somber moments in life (and there have been some of the latter). Beginning with small and very general things that we must all have felt were very real to us at some time or other, I have progressively drawn on private, lasting memories fixed forever in powerful mental images, dazzling snapshots of experience that can, I think, be conveyed in a few words. This essay should be seen as a kind of prose poem paying tribute to life.

It is true that I think I have not had too many problems in life. I have been lucky enough to deal, in my work, with intellectual questions that give depth and a singular touch of pleasure to everyday existence. I have enjoyed my work, and still do. I have also been lucky enough not to know poverty or, unlike millions of human beings today, enormous difficulty in simply surviving. What I have written here could therefore look like the hedonism of a woman who has led a privileged life. However, I will venture to think that, in describing pure sensuality, it evokes the actual experience of humanity in general.

The reader will become aware of the length of time involved. I was born before the Second World War, which made a great impression on me, although it did not entail much suffering on my own part. Indeed, it meant that during long holidays in this part of Auvergne that is now the Livradois National Park I became familiar with country life of a kind that is now in the past. I shall touch only lightly on the time I have spent in Africa and on my experience of illness. But many encounters will be found here, oddities, an attentive eye for nature and what it creates, for animals, noise, sounds, light and shade, aromas . . . and above all, other people.

The reader will not find glimpses of my private life in this essay, or very few of them. Nor will I dwell on the pleasures of the intellect, of research and writing, although those pleasures are intense. Or on love, although nonetheless it has played an important part in my life, as I suppose it will have done in those of readers. That was not my subject. What is it, then?

There is a kind of lightness and grace in the simple fact of existence, leaving aside our occupations, strong feelings, political and other commitments, and I wanted to confine my subject in this essay to that aspect. To the little plus factors that are granted to us all, and go to make up the flavor of life.

The

SWEETNESS

of

LIFE

I was delighted to get your postcard yesterday and know that you were taking a holiday in that lovely place, an island to make anyone dream. You sounded happy in the mists of Scotland. All the same, you didn't "steal" your holiday in the sense of pilfering or misappropriating property. Instead, I would say that you are stealing from your own life every day.

If you assume an average life expectation of 85 years, or 31,025 days, always having, also on average, 8 hours of sleep a day; if you spend 3 hours 30 minutes on shopping, preparing, and eating meals, washing up after them, and so on; 1 hour 30 minutes on personal hygiene and grooming, sickness, etc.; 3 hours on keeping the family going: children, transport, interaction with other people, DIY work, etc.; 140 hours of work a month for 45 years at a rate of 6 hours a day, not counting the pleasure that work may give you; 1 hour a day for obligatory social relationships, conversations with the neighbors, having a drink, meetings, seminars, and so on; then how much time is left for the average citizen, male or female, to enjoy those activities that are the sweetness of life?

Going on holiday, to the theater, the cinema, the opera, concerts, exhibitions, reading, listening to music or playing it, various ways of taking exercise, walking, going on excursions, travel, gardening, visits to friends, relaxing, writing, creative arts, dreaming, reflection, sports (all of them), board games and party games, in fact games of any kind, doing crossword puzzles, resting, conversation, friendship, flirtation, love, and why not add guilty pleasures as well? You'll notice that I haven't even mentioned sex. You'll never guess: in what we think of as the active or working period of our lives, you have 1 hour 30 minutes a day for all that, and between 5 and 7 hours after, because the time returned to the other tasks increases.

And there you go extending your working hours by taking time from everything else, and missing out on all those pleasant things to which our deepest selves aspire.

I left out a lot of things in my list of those that make up the sweetness of life. So I will go on, following the method of the Surrealists, by looking at associations of ideas and letting them come of their own accord. All this may strike you as hedonistic, since I have left out all the subtleties of intellectual pleasure, or what we feel in commitments—and you may not even think it very serious if I'm not going to mention sex. Nonetheless, some things are very serious and very necessary if we are to preserve our "zest" for life; I'm talking about the intimate thrill of small pleasures, I'm talking about questions and even setbacks if we give them time to exist. I will go on.

. . . I forgot about wild laughter, phone calls made for no real reason, handwritten letters, family meals (well, some of them), meals with friends, a beer at the bar, a glass of red or white wine, coffee in the sun, a siesta in the shade, eating oysters at the seaside or cherries straight from the tree, putting on a great show of anger, but only in pretense, making a collection (of stones, butterflies, boxes or cans, how would I know exactly what?), the bliss of fresh autumn evenings, sunsets, waking up at night when everyone's asleep, trying to remember the words of old songs, searching for smells or tastes, reading the newspaper in peace, looking through photograph albums, playing with a cat, building an imaginary house, setting a place at table attractively, drawing casually on a cigarette, keeping a diary, dancing (ah, dancing!), going out to parties, going to the ball on National Day, listening to the New Year concert like millions of others, lounging on a sofa, strolling along the streets and window-shopping, trying on shoes, clowning around and doing imitations, setting out to explore a city you don't know, playing football or Scrabble or dominoes, devising puns and plays on words, talking nonsense, cooking a complicated dish, going angling or jogging or playing bowls, thinking all around an idea, watching an old film on TV or in an experimental art-house cinema, whistling with your hands in your pockets, keeping your mind vacant, moments of silence and solitude, running in warm rain, long conversations at twilight, kisses on the back of the neck, the smell of warm croissants in the street, winks of complicity, the moment when all nature falls silent . . . listening to the happy cries of children at play, feasting on ice cream or chocolates, those moments when you know that someone likes you, is looking at you and listening to you, feeling agile and sprightly, sleeping in late in the morning, getting on board a fishing boat, watching a craftsman at work, stopping to listen to a smooth talker peddling his wares (my goodness, that was a long time ago!), enjoying the sight of street life, getting back together with friends you haven't seen for ages, really listening to other people . . .

And there's still so much else that I forget.

What about you, what would you miss most if all this had to disappear from your life forever?

I can tell that I risk boring you to tears.

. . . listening with fanatical enthusiasm to Mozart, the Beatles, Astrud Gilberto, going on a trip to Switzerland and back in a single night to be at a concert given by your favourite singer, gorging on Alpine strawberries, walking on coastal roads on a windy day, waiting up to see an eclipse or eagle owl flying by night, racking your brains to think what would please someone you love, walking barefoot, listening to voices echoing over the sea, stretching and yawning, switching on either just a small flashlight or large projectors, paying compliments when you're going out for a good time, catching glances that say a great deal, turning down the corner of a page even though that's not the proper thing to do, throwing politeness out of the window for a while, forgetting to pick up your mail, walking arm in arm or hand in hand with someone, going against the tide, holding the door open for an elegant old gentleman, curling up in a ball, breathing in the fresh air of early morning, watching branches shaken by the wind, lighting a crackling fire, stuffing yourself with sausage and pickled gherkins, waiting for the moment when an angel briefly passes by (at twenty minutes past, twenty minutes to, and on the hour), putting your foot in it in company, shaking your hair all over the place, smiling at someone who's not expecting it, talking seriously about a frivolous subject and joking about a serious one (but mind who you do it with!), not letting any louts or know-it-alls take you in, enjoying what you like without inhibitions (including the roar of racing cars), listening to the life in your own body, sleeping flat on your back, waving like Columbo, going upstairs four steps at a time, arriving somewhere out of breath, crying in the cinema, letting your emotions all hang out or alternatively preserving an Olympian calm, keeping quiet or admiring or listening, taking cycling or playing the piano or archery up again . . . using the luxurious restrooms of a grand hotel while out walking, sitting down in an armchair too deep for you, picking up incongruous little items, plunging your hands in the moss of a woodland floor or the foam of detergent, listening to the local policeman's drumroll (although they don't beat the drum these days) or barrel organs in the street (you don't get those either these days), racing your lover, sitting by an open window, waking up in a place you don't recognize, feeling your heart beat fast, weighing up arguments, testing the weight of a melon, seeing a childhood friend again, digging up buried memories (my God, yes, that's how it was!), taking your time over choosing some small thing (and deciding on important things in haste), following the flight of a single swallow among a flock of others, watching a cat from above when it doesn't know you're watching it, laughing up your sleeve, waiting for the twilight hour, watering your plants and talking to them, appreciating the touch of fine leather or a peach or someone's hair, studying the background of the *Mona Lisa* or the filigree effects of Vlaminck in detail, feeling pleasure at the sound of a voice, setting off for wherever the fancy takes you, staying in the dusk and doing nothing, cautiously trying grilled locusts, indulging in endless conversations with women friends of many years' standing, making up good stories . . .

I'll go on, at the risk of boring you, because all this is going to get more and more focused. I get the impression that I'm undermining banks already on the point of collapse. After all, I'm giving you ammunition for the day when, in twenty years' time, people ask you what I was like.

. . . whispering on the telephone, fixing dates years in advance, swooning over the bearing of Robert Mitchum, the way Henry Fonda walks, the smile of Brad Pitt, the romantic beauty of Gene Tierney and Michelle Pfeiffer, the ingenuous nature of Marilyn Monroe, the grace of Audrey Hepburn; enjoying a *coppo del nonno* coffee gelato in Florence, sighing with pleasure, walking round a big department store, driving on potholed tracks in a jeep, eating with your fingers while crouching on the ground round the dish, sharing a cola nut or chocolate bar, being scared in the cinema, reading thrillers or good SF, shamelessly taking the best peach out of the fruit bowl, carefully

extracting winkles from their shells, eating in a
real transport café with a check tablecloth, making crystal glasses ring, watching a good rugby
match, playing belote or rummy or the yam game
or Ludo or dominoes, being a bad sport among
other bad sports, protesting vehemently over
nothing to speak of, refusing to argue with angry
people (children included, and allowing yourself the luxury of glaring at them in shops), also
allowing yourself the luxury of taxis reserved in
advance and looking at the queues outside railway
stations (*suave mari magno* . . .), having an umbrella when you need one, a big enough umbrella
for several people, walking fast, trailing your feet
through dead leaves, smiling lovingly at your
grandmother's photograph, listening to owls by
night and crickets by day, picking a bunch of wild-
flowers from embankments, watching swathes of
mist drift by, following the course of a hare racing
over the fields or of Jean-Louis Trintignant round
the port of Nice in the film set there, trying to pin
down the moment when you fall asleep, feeling the
weight of your exhausted body in bed, sleeping on
someone's shoulder, joining in a public festival,

watching a good fireworks display, listening to
Callas singing or the wind moaning or hail patter-
ing down, watching the fire, eating a sandwich in
the street, walking on hot sand (but not too hot),
sipping a drink, playing with a bunch of keys,
urinating outdoors, being moved to tears, shouting for joy when you see a perfect shot at goal in
soccer, caressing, being caressed, kissing, being
kissed, hugging, being hugged (with love, complicity, affection), feeling full of drive, enthusiasm,
passion, feeling your heart leap, ignoring conven-
tions, admiring the young, having eyes bigger
than your stomach, being deliciously scared, feeling unwell and opening your eyes to see friendly
faces, enjoying an idea or a project or a memory
by yourself, going out on the tarmac in Niamey
in the rainy season and smelling the warm, spicy
odor of African soil, seeing a pair of lions silently
cross the trail in moonlight, taking an animal by
surprise when its eyes are transfixed in a vehicle's
headlights, talking all night, wanting to be sur-
rounded by happiness, clearing out your cup-
boards, feeling surprised that you are still alive,
being delighted when you suddenly find, in a flash,

the solution to a problem that has been bothering
you for ages, getting a present you like or a token
of friendship or a postcard, singing popular songs
in chorus, keeping secrets, conscientiously thinking up ideas, enjoying mild weather . . .

And there's more to come . . .

. . . melting over the devastating restraint of Robert Redford in *Out of Africa* and the equally devastating insolence of Clark Gable in *Gone With the Wind*; sorting lentils, taking a pebble out of your shoe, having a bath at midnight, seeing the Northern Lights, turning somersaults and cartwheels in the grass (that was a long time ago!), finding a four-leaved clover, getting a game of patience to come out, rediscovering a taste for recipes of the past, calculating how many steps you take between stones on the pavements, listening to the little tune that tells you when a train is coming in or leaving, imagining what you could make of an object or a house or a place, choosing bread with a good crisp crust, picking grass to feed the rabbits, watering the flowers, knitting a soft scarf, seeing the curtain rise at the theater when the lights go out and the noise of the audience dies down, just having time for a mouthful of a cocktail, crying while listening to *Die Winterreise*, going in search of the sources of rivers, paying a compliment to a woman you don't know in the street, getting the day, the week, or the month wrong in making a date, meeting again after twenty years as if you'd never been parted, wearing a perfume that makes you forget yourself, knowing how to forget yourself, playing to the gallery, picking up a child, protesting at his weight but not bothering him with silly questions, wondering where you were before you were born rather than what happens to you after death, crumpling up newspaper, cutting out pictures and making collages, taking off or coming down in a plane, looking enviously at dishes being served at the next table in a restaurant, watching passers-by and trying your hand at amateur psychology, waiting outside a café, telling yourself you ought to go to the gym, remembering to breathe deeply now and then, starting to learn the trombone from scratch, making mayonnaise or beating egg whites for Îles flottantes by hand, discovering a delicious exotic fruit, remembering your baby language or proverbs or useful scraps of knowledge, using surprisingly apt words, drinking when you're very thirsty, never being ashamed to be yourself . . .

. . . having an intimate conversation with a Siamese cat or a Brittany spaniel, sneezing seven times running, being first to spot the spire of Trégunc church, having a picnic with all the trappings, singing "Stormy Weather" like Lena Horne or "Over the Rainbow" like Judy Garland, trying to sing "Mexico" like Luis Mariano and failing to hit the high notes, losing yourself in John Ford's vast skies, flying above the African bush in a small aircraft, making stones bounce as they skim the water, trembling with impatience, feeling your taste buds react to ginger, touching the moist nose of a calf, finding mushrooms, picking wild bilberries, looking for seashells at low tide, looking at your kitchen or your bedroom or your office when you've straightened it out, turning odd words over in your mouth ("scullery," "antiphon," "mithridatic," "hapax legomenon" . . .), riding on a cable-car railway, jumping at the three blows announcing the start

of a performance in a French theater, playing
hide-and-seek, winning a small something in a
raffle in the country, feeling slightly scared in a
long tree-lined avenue by night, having a nice
shower, getting your head massaged, packing
your cases, putting the key in the lock, setting
off on a journey, fishing for crayfish with your
bare hands (there are no more of them), collecting edible snails (no more of them either!), lying on a chaise longue, waiting for the postman,
shouting to hear the echo, kicking a stone away,
picking a scab on your knee before the eyes of
your disgusted parents (that was all long ago!),
having once got eighteen out of twenty in math,
playing the harmonica or the Jew's harp, having the last word, making a wooden scale model,
finishing a big jigsaw puzzle, seeing Fujiyama
or Kilimanjaro from far away, wanting to go to
Bobo-Dioulasso, drinking in the words of someone you love, watching James Stewart in a good
western and seeing the train winding its way
over the plains with a one-armed Spencer Tracy
on board, flinching with horror in your seat in
front of *Alien* or a zombie film, watching a tama-

risk, going to sleep while having magnetic resonance imaging, cheering up the nurse who can't find a vein, finding the young physician on duty "irresistible," getting told off by a Swiss from Lausanne for crossing the road when the light is green but the little man is red, putting your hands in your pockets, jumping and bouncing on a bed (that was a long time ago too), taking an artichoke apart, spinning out a metaphor, finding good sunglasses, choking on a strong piri-piri pepper, giving a sharp reply if you have to, taming an animal, scanning the horizon in search of the island that you see only when it's going to rain, sweating blood over something you're writing, and water when cycling uphill . . .

. . . going to a lot of trouble over nothing much, striking matches, polishing copper until it shines, dozing in a boring meeting, doing cryptic cross-word puzzles, swearing like a trooper at things that keep getting in your way, not being taken in by pointed and flattering attentions, succumb-ing to greed, climbing the towers of Notre-Dame and dreaming of going to Machu Picchu, feeling the spray of Niagara Falls blown sideways into your face, walking all round an enormous baobab tree, drawing water from a well by the strength of your arms alone, without a pulley, enjoying the protection of a mosquito net, opening a gift pack-age (what can be in it?), admiring a large Poitou donkey or Salers cow, throwing yourself on your bed in exhaustion with a sense of duty done, fin-ishing a major washing-up session, climbing mountains in misty weather, in fine weather, and in a cold wind, opening the hood of a car with steam coming out of it in the high mountain pass

Casse Déserte de l'Izoard (this was on the verge of the 1950s), finding an old box of treasures with a fine piece of mica in it, being aware of the transience of things and the necessity of seizing your chance, reciting a La Fontaine fable with feeling, overcoming idleness and fear of change, drinking a beer on a terrace late on a fine afternoon, shivering slightly as evening comes on, being impervious to the treacherous nature of some propositions, passing unnoticed when those who rule the roost are raking money in, failing to admire Mr. Muscles and his biceps, leading a goat by its horns, being sworn at by a jealous Siamese cat, identifying instruments when you don't know what they are for, keeping quiet and speaking only after careful consideration, not feeling obliged to do the same as everyone else, wondering if the monastic life would be worth trying, being curious about everything, keeping your eyes open, happily breathing in the smell of new-mown hay or kelp, not so sure about the smell of mud at low tide, fording a river or crossing it on stepping-stones, drawing a mustache on the *Mona Lisa* (and laughing secretly when you remember Marcel Duchamp's surrealist version of her), keeping so quiet that you deceive a bird, catching a fly in one hand like Obama, hearing the cascading of a waterfall, screaming blue murder when you sit down in a car heated by the sun . . .

. . . getting a guinea fowl or any other creature as a present still alive and kicking, having plenty of boxes, lofts, and roomy wardrobes, standing on the edge of a sheer drop, imitating the voices, movements, and intonations of people or animals to perfection, going to bed in sheets that have just been changed, sanctimoniously contemplating bucolic frescos, doing your nails, getting up and saying no, putting your heart into a piece of work, laughing with Coluche and Desproges, Chaplin and Keaton, standing lost in baffled thought in front of certain "works of art," utterly refusing to have certain books on your shelves (for instance any by xenophobic writers and Holocaust deniers), feeling at ease, even if fleetingly, in body and mind . . . finding a substitute for a flawed tool, reciting the list of all the French departments and their capitals (am not so sure of some of them!), laughing your head off at female fashions of the 1930s but liking those of ancient Crete, seeing the first irises come into bloom, lovingly cutting cosmos flowers for the house, raking up dead leaves, bringing in the hay, appreciating the quality of silence after an orgy of sound, feeling surprised and moved by evidence of the past, beginning to read the newspaper at the back page, laughing at the crazy consequences of confusing right and left when reading a map, going out in the car before or after everyone else, or driving against the main flow of traffic and enjoying the illusion of being all-powerful, boiling an egg in an enormous pan (like Keaton), refraining for once from coming up with a witty retort only after the event . . .

Is that the end?

. . . making a blade of grass between your fingers and your lips whistle, listening in bed at night to the Westminster chimes extending their *ritornello* every quarter of an hour in the kitchen at Bodélio, hearing the sound buoy of Moelan "moo," seeing a great stampede in a western, stroking the soft, faded skin of an old lady's hands, calling your mother "my little mother," your daughter "my treasure," your husband "my heart" and feeling to the full how accurate those descriptions are, dining in a restaurant in an inner courtyard in a country town, enjoying a funny rabbinical joke, singing *"Quand on s'promène au bord de l'eau"* along with Jean Gabin, knowing how to pronounce the name of the town of Cunlhat properly, opening a letter with your heart racing, being out of doors when the devil marries his daughters (what? Oh, sorry, meaning out in a shower on an otherwise fine day), foretelling that it will rain tomorrow from the angle of the rays of the setting sun, solemnly calling a teenage boy Monsieur, listening to the sweet voice of Rina Ketty singing *"J'attendrai"* as she waits for her man to come back and the piquant voice of Mireille in her song about *ce petit chemin*; skipping around with Charles Trenet and, with Yves Montand, looking at the legs of the girl on a swing; for the first time and with some inner trepidation using the Christian name of someone you revere and who has expressed a wish to be on first-name terms with you, waking up in Paris to the music of Jacques Dutronc, conscientiously licking the plate clean, sitting in the sun in the Piazza Navona in Rome in February while you eat a rocket salad and drink a glass of Orvieto, holding buttercups under your chin to see if there's a yellow reflection, eating grapes straight from the trellis on the front of a house, seeing large raindrops splash down on the ground, or a huge rainbow, or a distant light in the dark night sky, or a shooting star or, very high up, a space capsule silently passing; having a piggy bank, a talisman, a slender waist, surprising an animal going about its own business, feeling the density of an attentive silence, entering a conversation as you might enter the arena, finding the right word for something at last, waiting for a phone call, feeling sorry that pebbles lose their beautiful colors as they dry, entertaining the fantasy of a big house with green shutters standing at a crossroads in the heart of a forest, admiring the entrance of a house reached by two elegant flights of steps, or opulent hollyhocks or a porch roofed with glazed tiles, singing a cappella and in unison, vibrating at the sound of a voice, being struck directly by troubling likenesses and acting with a newcomer as you would with an old acquaintance, talking to yourself in private, loyally retaining a certain idea of those you have loved, getting the proofs of a new book, eating wild honey from combs gathered by smoking the bees out, crunching radishes, making apple compote and shortcrust pastry tarts, drinking fresh cider, sleeping out of doors, admiring the nocturnal labors of termites under shoes left on the floor of a hut, drinking warm millet beer from a calabash and passing it to your neighbor, going for a long drive along a rough track without puncturing a tire; seeing the white coat of the medical supervisor you are waiting for in his hospital department at the end of the corridor, as he stalks along like a tall heron in a hurry, and feeling comforted, full of joy and well-being; loving all of life during fieldwork, even in discomfort, striking up a conversation easily, coming to terms with what you hate, herding cows, drawing wine from a cask, watching the fingertips of your doctor's expert hands as they identify what's wrong, artlessly saying something funny and paying attention only to your audience's laughter, going all the way down a long steep street in a car without stopping at the crossroads someday, going to the hairdresser's, having a manicure . . .

This is addictive. I'll go on.

. . . keeping perfectly still in front of a black mamba that has not woken up properly, loving *House* and the goth girl with black bunches in *NCIS* and the character of Ally McBeal, skipping a rope held by two girlfriends turning it faster and faster (that was back in prehistory), enjoying a gin fizz with the rim of the glass frosted or a Campari and soda, eating pistachio and cashew nuts one after another, dipping a sugar lump in your neighbor's coffee cup, scraping up the sugary residue from the bottom of the cup, surviving the attack of a swarm of wild bees in the African bush, breathing in the powerful odor of hot tar or the faintly nauseating smell of the manufacturing of shea butter, swerving athletically to avoid ruts too deep for your tyres, imagining the underside of crinoline dresses, listing all sorts of loincloths for men, managing to haul yourself back into a hospital bed on your own, knowing that the man

you are waiting for will come, seeing the land-
scape opening out like a corolla from the top of
a hill, feeling the earth turn beneath your feet
while you watch the clouds . . . calculating the
time between lightning and thunder, scrutinizing
the darkness and seeing strange snaky shapes like
lamias there, making people think you can read
the future in coffee grounds, trying to get a game
of cards to work out, coming back in triumph
from a cookery class one day, after learning to
make celéry rémoulade, and stuffing the family
with it for days; remembering the shame of faux
pas committed in the past, going to midnight
mass at the church of St. Augustin and sliding
along the rue du Général Foy, its frozen surface
still wooden at the time; having been very good
at putting the shot and no other kind of sport
at all; trying to work out what deserved a great
historian's congratulations before realizing that
he was talking about himself; wearing a pretty
red dress to the wedding of a friend, the son of
an ambassador to the USSR (that dates me), to
a novelist who was already famous; cycling fast
up slopes like Gino Bartali in the Tour de France

but braking hard on the way down; laughing in a bumper car although you hated it, going on the dance floor with only an accordionist and a drummer, waltzing wonderfully well but also liking to dance the java, the rumba, the paso doble, the tango, even rock (yes, I did!), sitting up all night to finish reading a novel, sitting up all night with the first death in my family (of the mother of my mother's mother), sitting up all night with a baby, hearing a little tune by Mozart that always makes the heart turn over, falling off a platform in front of a hundred people, getting up and going on as if nothing had happened, playing the "What if?" game; paddling in the sea, touching sensitive plants, carefully picking cactus fruits, stroking a tame hedgehog, having a pet sheep called Pedro, watching the cat Petite Demoiselle fight a rat in a granary (the cat won), eating on one and the same day in Livradois warm rye bread cut up in a tart, potatoes "for the pigs" cooked in a big pan, freshly churned butter, and cake with black cherries (this was in the war, and it could have been yesterday), remembering the wartime radio programme *Ici Londres* and seeing the maquisard Resistance fighters in Auvergne, sheltering in cellars during air raids on Saint-Étienne, Firminy, La Ricamarie, Rive-de-Gier, loving the brownish sugar that melted in compote dishes and potato cakes (a thick, filling dish), watching the great meeting of the political Left at the gates of Versailles with François Mitterrand, Georges Marchais, and Robert Fabre, hearing the news of the French May 1968 protests when I was in the bush over a crackling transistor radio brought by an immigrant from Ghana; reacting violently to the opulence of our shopping streets on my return from ascetic periods in Africa, attending several meetings of the emergent Movement for the Liberation of Women (MLF) near Montsouris Park; keeping everything I have been given, helpfully giving information to tourists and people who had lost their way so that I was late myself; writing by hand, being obsessed for a while with an encounter yet to come or the precise point of an argument yet to be settled or the best way of setting out an idea; making tea, organizing an impromptu dinner, returning to consciousness in a recovery room after being in a coma and thinking briefly that this was the end of me; being happy when your child is happy, soaking up feelings, feeling everything strongly but not letting it show . . . having no more toothache (or any other kind of ache), making a door or a step on the stairs or chalk on a slate squeal, picturing everything very clearly in the imagination, treasuring the ugly photo of my mother in a cycling jersey posing beside her bike for the local paper at the age of over sixty after an amateur cycle race, feeling incapable of such an achievement, always doubting my own abilities and worrying about the veracity of praise that I have received (how well trained in modesty we were!); knowing my star sign as Scorpio with Cancer in the ascendant and reading horoscopes with amusement; getting annoyed with the titles that newspapers impose on interviews or on articles you send them, feeling satisfaction at hoarding two-euro coins away in a box so as not to be caught without cash; retaining ever since the days of rationing a terror of going short, worrying about running out of petrol and still having to find the hotel before nightfall, particularly with children in the car; waiting for my daughter outside school or making her a snack to take, exchanging letters with her containing clumsy drawings by both parties, playing at Sleeping Beauty with her, laughing at ads claiming "I wouldn't do this every day," finding myself unable to remember funny stories, trusting my brother and never getting bored by him; avoiding weightiness without giving up your own point of view, hating a curt tone of voice, stiff, coarse, offensive manners, disdainful looks, the lack of consideration for others that you find in those who, for some reason, think themselves superior; always talking and acting in the same way, in the same tone of voice and the same language, in front of everyone; considering that the word "kindness" denotes a great virtue, not looking away from adversity, regarding friendship as a commitment, getting absorbed in watching an anthill at work, walking into a field to make the grasshoppers leap out, knowing where red squirrels nest, having large keys to the barred gates in your garden, letting weeds grow between the paving stones of a terrace, being unable to do without nasturtiums in the garden, making a ladybug walk on your finger, watching milk on the stove and taking it off the heat just in time, making a chocolate mousse to my mother's old recipe (with butter in it), still feeling nostalgic about poached eggs in red wine sauce, being naively astonished by conjuring tricks, being dazzled by a fine sight and captivated by a good speech . . .

. . . being invited to the country by friends you are fond of and discovering that the ocean lies just beyond their house, and there's the priest's garden with its orchard and cottage-garden flowers; admiring your great-uncle's handsome mustache in the Vercingetorix style and your old cousin's grating voice (the result of being gassed in 1914), which resembles the voice of historian Henri-Irénée Marrou after tracheotomy; enjoying coffee (with milk for those who like it white) and sharing biscuits with your cousin's dogs and cats who sit like good children around the big table; stretching out at length with your hands behind your head and your feet on the coffee table (sad to say I can't prop mine on a desk as characters do in old American films), hoping to succeed in striking a match on the sole of your shoe someday or hold a revolver, metaphorically speaking, like Humphrey Bogart, watching *Butch Cassidy and the Sundance Kid* again, also *Kiss Me Deadly*, *The Incredible*

Shrinking Man, *A High Wind in Jamaica*, and *The Dead*; remembering listening conscientiously to the daily 5 P.M. reading from Molly Bloom's monologue on Europe 1 (which could almost be called a cultural radio channel in its early stages); having a horror of deadlines, leafing through catalogues like those of the Manufrance mail-order firm (I was told that at the age of three I meticulously studied every picture as I turned its pages), inhaling the smell of a book little by little before beginning to reread it from the first to the last line, provided that it made a good first impression, discovering new words (one of mine is the slightly suspect but marvellous "procrastination," picked up rather late in life!), shedding tears in front of the TV set when the cheetah in the animal documentary discovers his mortally wounded brother and prowls around him, scolding him, while the wounded creature follows him with his eyes, groaning like a human child . . . waiting for the moment in the film *The Bear* when the bear draws himself up to his full height in front of Tchéky Karyo, playing the part of the hunter, who is paralyzed by fear and humility; being surprised to

find Leonardo DiCaprio playing a simpleminded
adolescent with a nervous laugh who dreams only
of climbing to the top of the water tower, and
Robert De Niro talking to himself in his little
room ("you talkin' to me?"); coming out of the
Métro on an empty platform, running through a
heavy thunderstorm and taking refuge, laughing,
under an awning; tasting salty caramel; going
through a forest or a huge park full of *balanẓan*
trees, or a desert, or salt marshes or mangrove
swamps or the Dombes region near Lyon, wondering about the shape or color of an artichoke
flower or a eucalyptus seed, trying to imagine the
long journey taken by the voice that reaches you
all the way from Sydney; fuming with impatience
as things pile up to make you late (staying in bed
too long, no taxi, traffic congestion . . .); watching
the work of an itinerant farrier, seeing donkeys
and goats pass by with their little bells on their
way back from the Jardin du Luxembourg, or the
Republican Guard on horseback, or a procession
of vintage cars all going out on a country road;
picking mulberries, escaping an angry bull or a
discontented goose or a watchdog, watching with

annoyance as the tongues of interested cows snap up the fine mushrooms you were going to pick, blushing and being cross with yourself for it, loving someone who has no idea of it . . . sharing your plate in a restaurant, ordering a dish at random when you're abroad, polishing up an old wardrobe, never tiring of listening to Miles Davis or Thelonious Monk, putting a misogynist in his place by using his own range of expressions, pouring orange-flower water into your maternal grandmother's glass out of pure kindness, only to find her surprised later by the strange flavor of the wine: "I assure you, Étienne (her son-in-law), this wine is truly undrinkable!," being surprised to find yourself connected, during a phone call, to a conversation with strangers, listening to your grandmothers talk family matters at length, marveling at pictures by Hokusai or calligraphy or Portuguese *azulejos* tiles or grass skirts, having a basket full of African bracelets . . .

. . . dreading an untimely scarlet stain on your white trousers, avoiding any such danger and going home in good time, drinking from the bottle or without letting your lips touch its rim, placing a round loaf upside down and remembering ancestral reproaches: "That's no way to earn your bread" (i.e., lying idle on your back), arranging fruit in a basket, being in a car with tinted windows so that you can't be seen from outside, opening a bottle with a corkscrew and making the cork vibrate with a "plop," collecting glowworms, catching the scent of your grandmother's eau de cologne in the street, admiring the dresses worn by the heroine of the fairy-tale musical film *Peau d'âne*, dreaming of having the long, slender legs and melancholy look of Italian madonnas with the baby Jesus on their knees or the artistic blond pallor of Tilda Swinton, feeling I wanted to die on the spot the day—long ago now—when Claude Lévi-Strauss asked out of the blue if I had

any comment to make after a lecture by someone
else that I had not understood and promising myself never to put anyone else in the same position,
carefully choosing a bracelet for a woman friend,
comforting a soul in pain, being given marrons
glacés, to have seen Cocteau's *The Eagle Has
Two Heads* at the Théâtre Hébertot with Edwige
Feuillère and Jean Marais, who could have looked
ridiculous but didn't in leather trousers with sus-
penders, picking daffodils once in a forest near
Paris, being close one day to the strong odor of a
real billy goat, spending hours studying the two
classic chromolithographs of the Ages of Life, to
have been captivated by the beauty of my father's
large, flexible hands; inhaling at length, with
eyes closed, the secret aroma of tar and the sea
in the hair of a beloved person who allows you
to do so, drawing a pretty blue line at the corners
of your eyes; being taken by surprise when a girl
said, with tears in her eyes, how moved she is to
meet you, trying to surprise a snail by touching
its feelers, inadvertently giving yourself an elec-
tric shock in the elbow, admiring the fine looks
of a group of adolescent girls, falling into ecsta-

sies over the color and transient form of a hibiscus flower, considering that because of our fixed ideas of the number forty you are older at forty than at fifty or sixty, worrying, being afraid of committing a faux pas or of a delay or of what people will say, attracting the attention of someone whose approval you want, being ridiculously pleased with what you have just done . . .

. . . never to have read certain great writers but remembering with delight the mysterious word "*morne*" that I found in the West Indies of my first real children's book, spending two months in a boarding school for deaf-mutes while my brother was suffering from scarlet fever, enjoying solitude and avoiding too effervescent an atmosphere, seeing likenesses without ever being able to draw, reviving the dead by talking about them, excoriating yourself mentally for cowardice, laziness, vacillation and uncertainty, lack of a sense of coherence, susceptibility, slowness, greed, a propensity for putting things off until tomorrow, fear of disturbing other people, and many more faults, coming upon the adjective "suspicious" used by a friend to explain why his emotional experiences ended badly, which made me wonder how anyone can live without trust; feeling at times, when pain went away, a sense of absolute happiness that goes to the heart

and almost hurts; knowing someone so indiffer-
ent to everyday life that he has to look out of the
window if he is asked on the phone if it is fine
or raining, mentally adopting my grandmother's
unsparing judgments and pithy epithets: a stuck-
up female, a total idiot, a halfwit, a gossip, a
bragger, a belligerent, a fatso, a virago, a clumsy
clot, someone always trying to piss higher than
last time, a happy imbecile, a hussy, the wrong
sort, an old dragon, a great goof, a pain in the
neck, a real tart, a bad penny, a proper little
madam, a down-and-out, someone who knocks
around, all of which bears witness to her moral
ideas and her conception of "gender"! . . . also
being up in arms, figuratively speaking, when
an adult puts you in the same category as his
grandparents—oh, and what else is there? . . .
being glad to have few wrinkles but bothered by
ugly scars; admiring newborn babies, their tiny
hands, their round eyes, their perfectly formed
mouths, all those parts into which knowledge
and love will pass; going to the Easter lamb and
kid fair sometimes, liking the market, the fresh
eyes of a fish, the mounds of fruit, great blocks of

Cantal cheese, the herb stall; listing with delight the wealth of hardware and haberdashery and trimmings available, trembling with joy at the idea of giving someone a nice surprise, telling stories, reading aloud; loving four cats at various times: Roulette, a timid cat from the Auvergne with gray fur; Julie, a demanding and voluble blue-point Siamese; Petite Mère, a knowing tabby from Brittany, and her son Mitchum, a sweet, paler tabby with a handsome chest; never having managed to satisfy the appetite of a greedy nanny goat called Aglae, not even with forty-eight apple turnovers, pains au chocolat with raisins, palmier biscuits and brioches; and as a child (together with my sister and our girl cousin) getting an old and very rustic nanny goat drunk on rum-cream dessert . . .

. . . collecting the full set of the *Cahiers du cinéma*, regretting that I don't look good in a hat, liking to wear first red and then black and now blue, sobbing in silence for hours looking at the human figures like "black commas" falling from the Twin Towers on September 11, loving old toys that get put away again, always searching (although in vain) for the real taste of Reinette apples from Le Mans, or stoned apricots tasting of honey, or vineyard peaches or gooseberries, uninhibitedly using words and expressions that are family inventions: the air here is very "soapoforic," don't cast "nasturtiums" on him . . . giving up when faced with picture puzzles and guessing games, sometimes remaining naive and not minding; flying off the handle when someone said of Simone de Beauvoir's *The Second Sex* that it "wasn't bad for a woman" and putting him in his insignificant place with a few well-chosen words; going down the great avenue in Bodélio park in the time of its splendor before the great storm struck, once knowing a cat who vociferously demanded to be let out when a little girl took her violin out of its case . . . laughing uproariously at my father imitating the gorilla and then with fear at the opening scene of Mario Bava's horror film *Black Sunday*, suffering nightmares for ages because of Radot's *The Wolf of the Malveneurs*; being able to laugh my head off or weeping my eyes out simply by thinking of something, feeling serenely at home in the internal medicine department of La Pitié hospital, having had my wrists tied when I had chickenpox so as not to scratch myself, herding cows while making rosaries, riding as a child on the back of the big shepherd dog Bijou, hitting out at roosters which to childish eyes were attacking harmless hens when they jumped on them, regretting never having seen a woman giving birth or indeed any other creature, even my cat Julie kittening, dining on excellent local charcuterie, then an Auvergnat dish of bacon and all the vegetables, then pigeons with peas, then a jugged hare ("I'm acquainted with that hare," said the cousin who had snared it), then roast veal from the local butcher with small round potatoes fried in walnut oil and big white Soissons haricot beans, followed by salad, and then the house's goat cheese, and then pears in wine with biscuits and then an apple tart (phew!) with coffee and a glass of the local spirits, all extensively and lavishly garnished; emerging from a long period of ill health resembling a tornado and telling myself it must be fine outside, trying to pacify a woman who was disturbed and calling for the nurse all night; feeling carried away by a heavy, rhythmic swell at sea and forgetting that everything is finite, groping about in search of a flashlight (which didn't work), remembering, decades later, a simple organdie dress that felt scratchy, hesitating to put my hand under a stone after seeing *The Treasure of the Sierra Madre*, and casually throwing an envelope with my name and address on it in a waste bin in the street after reading Patricia Highsmith; thinking of the workings of chance that mean we are not contemporaries of people we would like to have known, telling yourself that a lion with a thorn in its paw or hedgehog spines in its nose must feel really hand-

icapped, hearing your own voice over a loud-
speaker, enjoying the atmosphere of the
graveyards of little towns on All Saints' Day, seeing Frankenstein in person, otherwise known as
the gravedigger, emerging from the graveyard;
to have looked after litters of kittens and superflu-
ous piglets who were suckled by a goat, remembering strolling along brilliant streets, wondering
with concern what we would have done in cir-
cumstances that in fact we were spared . . . en-
gaging in hopeless battles with the castors of
trolleys and mobile drips, hating the resistance of
inanimate objects; assessing the difference in
perception of the past between your own memories and those of your brother and sister, husband, daughter, marveling at the ability of the
human species to adapt, seething inside at some
people's cheerful stupidity or childishness or
self-importance or cowardice or malice, refusing
to speak a provincial language, blushing at my
pronunciation of English, imagining people's
characters from their voices, pitying those stars
of the silent screen who, like John Gilbert, had
falsetto voices and whose careers therefore came

to a sudden end, liking voices that are deep or
hesitant or precise or warm or laughing or sweet
or have a catch in them, and attributing a phy-
sique and a never-changing age to each voice;
relishing the sound in your mouth of a sparkling
word like "ampersand" or the mischief of "chari-
vari" or the grotesque "rookie" for a soldier or
the skittish "Trastevere" or the emphasis of "dis-
tinguished salutations" or the nostalgic sound of
"souvenir" . . . coming back from Italy in a con-
vertible yellow Fiat, rebelling against stupidity at
the right moment, opening shutters and windows
wide to let in currents of air, shivering with a
sense of having caught a chill, jumping at the
sound of doors slamming, seeing sheets put out to
dry blowing in the wind, admiring the beautiful
wisteria on certain houses, feeling happy to find
that everywhere, or almost everywhere, the
placid facades of our railway stations are made to
the same design, liking the look of windmills,
great birds that sometimes threaten to injure birds
of flesh and blood; being fundamentally, radi-
cally, quietly happy to be of my own sex but liking the opposite sex as well, finding a nest of gray

mice in the bed the day after coming home from months of absence, getting cross with the dormice ensconced above the ceiling, watching impotently as crows attack a tawny owl's nest, putting out dishes of fat and seeds for the birds in the trees in winter and finding them empty in spring, enduring the Harmattan trade wind of West Africa that dries your lips and burns your lungs, sharing the childish joy of being out in the first warm rains of June, seeing a Mercedes without wheels that is now a toy for the children of the Yatenga Naba, king of Waiguiyua, in a yard with mud walls in Burkina Faso, being palpated intimately at close quarters by the dry, intrusive hands of old ladies who came out of the bush to discover what sex this peculiar person was; wanting in the past to look like Simone Simon, being too short for my liking, being dismayed by the stupid opulence of the tall, disliking baths, fearing the results of having my hair cut at the hairdresser's unless Stéphanie does it, enjoying the epistolary novel in such titles as Mary Ann Shaffer and Annie Barrows' *The Guernsey Literary and Potato Peel Pie Society*, liking things that mur-

mur, whisper, reach the ear like drops of crystal
running down stalactites, living faithful to your
own ideas, friends, and loves, having moods of
enthusiasm but also of uneasiness, eating a supper
of pig's ears after the theater, hating the atmosphere at the sales, trying to catch yourself snor-
ing, being transported by joy after winning a little
victory over the way to use my Apple Mac, discovering that a driving license was the most diffi-
cult and thus the most gratifying certificate that I
ever gained, enjoying the company of women
friends, cherishing photographs and such small
things like the apple of my eye, eating a chocolate
in two mouthfuls as a reward for a great effort or a
victory, catching rainwater to rinse the hair, enjoying running after the bus to catch it by jumping on the back platform when the conductor
lifted the chain, planting a big kiss on the nose of
a cat who took offense, making a date with someone I loved at the other end of the world, but
specifying just where very precisely (and in six
months' time) and then not finding the place
(which no longer existed), but although mobiles
were not yet in use finding it all the same; keeping

a list of everywhere you happen to have slept on a
journey, going away with a companion at least
once a month so that the two of you can discover
new places, trying to follow a conversation in a
foreign language in which words of your own
surface now and then, liking cave dwellings
wherever they are, not really caring for the im-
personal voices at airports, triumphantly going
down the sunny side of the street in pink trousers
one fine April morning, feeling sudden outbursts
of joy as you might feel fits of heat, peeling *scorzo-
nera* and finding they turn your fingers black, addressing yourself to a face you have picked out in
an audience, being terribly afraid of being kept
waiting for a long time by those you love, rolling
up your sleeves in the real as well as the figurative
sense, catching a ball in the air, candling eggs,
peeling sweet chestnuts, relishing complicated
family trees and remembering other people's as
well as you remember your own, liking large
puppets, being crazy for West Coast jazz and Bix
Beiderbecke, the "young man with a horn," getting lost in Saenredam's tall white churches with
their high aisles and heavy doors, standing trans-

fixed in front of the thick paste of Van Gogh's vi-
olet irises, to have dined at the famous three-star
Troisgros restaurant when there really were three
of the family running it, eating liquorice, eating
millet porridge with a sauce of fresh baobab
leaves, finding a misprint on the fourth reading of
a proof, reading accounts of snowstorms, sitting
doing nothing, hands dangling, looking into
space, appreciating the beauty of cranes on a
building site at rest, of industrial landscapes and
disused railways, being cross with myself for
talking too fast or wanting to finish sentences for
people who speak slowly, applauding the successful backward passes of the wide line of attacking
players racing forward at a time when rugby really was an attacking game, living for long periods in an African hut made of the fermented mud
called banco, buying rustic plates in Cambridge
market, appreciating at its true value the venom-
ous hissing of Agnes Moorehead before she goes
out of the window in *Dark Passage*, seeing out of
the corner of an eye a small gray mouse scurry-
ing furtively into the kitchen in the country, tack-
ing in a felucca while sailing on the Nile and

seeing the work done on the project to rescue the temples on the island of Philae; remembering the ugliness of an enormous monkfish in the port of Marettimo and of staying there as a moment of grace, picturing Earth rushing through space under your body lying flat in a meadow covered with daisies, eating courgette-flower fritters, and in childhood consuming heart-shaped waffles made one by one in an adjustable black waffle iron on the heat of ancient cookers, holding back the tears at the first words of my inaugural lecture, getting Umberto Eco invited to the European Chair of the College of France and thus, in front of a large audience, forcing the minister responsible to take note of the striking absence of lecture rooms worthy of the name in that institution (we do now have the Marguerite de Navarre lecture hall); having seen Jean Vauthier's play *La nouvelle mandragore* from the raised seats on stage at the Théâtre de Chaillot and then approaching the legendary Gérard Philipe; watching the moon shine brightly in a sky full of luminous clouds, remembering the great jazz age days of the Café Tournon, of Richard Wright, of Chester Himes

(Coffin Ed and Gravedigger Jones) and Slim, remembering the postwar Christian Dior dresses with
swirling flared skirts and cinched waists; loving the
films of François Truffaut and the very individual
voice of Delphine Seyrig, to have traveled by
Caravelle airliner, stopping off three times on the
flight to Ouagadougou, waiting two years for a
phone line to be installed, remembering mail sent
by pneumatic tube, the death of a pope two
months after his election, the pleasure of walking
down the rue de la Huchette to go to Maspero or
the Caveau to listen to jazz, seeing Miles Davis,
all those anodyne things that have become the
mark of an era, loving words, the feel of them in
the mouth, their sonority, owning large numbers
of scarves that never get worn, inheriting six
crystal glasses, featuring as a birthday present
given by loving parents to their daughter when I
agreed to see her, having my opinions strengthened by letters from unknown admirers, spending hours in conversation with Francis who is
clever and attentive; playing at the children's
character of *la petite bête qui monte qui monte* with
my baby in fits of laughter, seeing Corpus Christi

processions with sheets at the windows and baskets of rose petals, remembering a cousin who milked her cows by hand with a clothes peg on her nose, seeing babies grow while old people shrink, amusing myself by talking in alexandrines, relishing the "sweetness of Anjou," living at one time above the Gare Montparnasse and feeling as if I were facing the transatlantic liner in *Amarcord* with all its portholes lit up, having big cuddles, amazement at the eroticism of the silent film *Queen Kelly* and the blazing eloquence of Daniel Day-Lewis in *The Age of Innocence*, enjoying the preciosity of David Suchet as Hercule Poirot as much as the rough-and-ready approach of Lino Ventura or the perversity of a sniggering Richard Widmark or the astonishing gentleness of Gene Tierney in *The Ghost and Mrs. Muir*, melting at the awkward look of Henry Fonda when told to dance the waltz in the final ball of *My Darling Clementine* . . .

. . . enjoying the austere world of *Dune* and its subterranean cathedrals of water, visiting the Montsouris reservoir, trying to revive a thrush that killed itself colliding with a windowpane and seeing the distress of the bird's partner who came back to the scene several days running; tinkering with old furniture, repainting a large room with the help of friends and relations, feeling at ease in the delicate architecture of the Great Mosque of Cordoba, admiring the huge black-bull silhouettes along the roads of Spain, picking a bunch of foxgloves, being present, frozen and drenched, at the bicentenary celebrations of the Revolution on the platforms in the place de la Concorde where the wind blew water from the fountains over the guests, always feeling particularly moved by a tiny church standing on its green esplanade, declining to eat cucumbers with cream and chantilly cream in general, loving municipal brass bands and watching end-of-the-year school shows, meeting the handsome bullfighter Luis Miguel Dominguín in his glory days, seeing strong minds weep at the death of Michel Foucault, sleeping in prickly hay, being a spectator at the full Christmas dinner given by the café proprietor who was mayor of Bertignat and his wife to a genuine vagabond wearing a huntsman's pouch and laced boots, who asked only for hot water and salt to cook his vermicelli and a glass of wine (he got two), to have heard some wonderful speakers, to have felt deeply confused as I raised an old lady from her knees while she begged me to make sure that her baby grandchild was cared for after her daughter had died in childbirth (I complied with her request) . . . driving on African roads like corrugated iron which were sure to ruin vehicles failing to reach the requisite speed, and following the fine tracks left by bicycle wheels tracing a zigzag course around natural obstacles on dusty or lateritic ground; feeling (mistakenly) sure of imminent death, trying to write legibly, dreaming of an attractive Yves Saint-Laurent pair of trousers for evening wear or a wonderful dress seen in a magazine, being astonished by the subject for a thesis about the "adhesive capacity of hairs on the front legs of a Madagascar spider," swooning at the sight of the lovesick King Kong but wondering how on earth anyone ever got him back into the ship's hold, spitting out grape or orange or mandarin or watermelon seeds or apple pips (we can forget about avocado stones), getting to the heart of the subject, analyzing a complex theme with precision, adding the final full stop to a text, seeing a deserted café standing up to the weather on the road, remembering, with a wry smile, having lessons in the social graces at school at the age of twelve or thirteen, almost drowning myself while laughing too loudly, crashing into two stationary cars coming out of a garage, remembering with emotion all my returns to the field in Africa, learning to take my bearings by the Pleiades, driving for hours through the thorny African bush, seeing that strange animal the aardvark, spending a whole night dripping with water under a clay roof that was dissolving in the rain, knowing some hidden springs, recollecting with pleasure those few encounters that have really made their mark on me, rejoicing secretly when something turns out exactly as foreseen, deciding that there's a touch of chill in the air and it would be a good idea to put on a jumper, marveling at the way people around you are getting younger whilst taking lessons from a twenty-five-year-old teacher of computer technology, feeling moved by my mother's dictum that she always felt twenty inside herself, and by the failure of my own father to recognize me, rediscovering the macaroon smell of gorse every summer, going to pick bilberries in the woods and coming back with lips stained black, feeling pain gently slip away when morphine takes effect, being crazy about the Robert Graves works based on Greek mythology, knowing that one way or another I have always been at school, living sparingly at the time of the Suez Crisis on a thin baguette and a cup of coffee a day and, with gratitude, dining one evening with a girlfriend's parents who were diamond merchants, receiving a proposal of marriage in Djerba from a local Tunisian who was fascinated by high-necked dresses, greeting the *hogon*, priest of the Dogon

people, outside the tall facade of his house with
its regularly spaced niches to hold animal skulls,
spending hours admiring the minute details of
relief maps of the cities of North Africa, going
on a cruise with a woman friend, riding a drome-
dary on one occasion, liking Turkish delight and
honey pastries, listening to the calls of crows in
the Indian Museum in Ottawa, laughing again at
the memory of a kitten seen at a roadside in Togo
eating pieces of chili-flavored meat voraciously
but with its fur bristling, remembering the swal-
lows in the sky of Paris and the amusement park
that went from Clichy to Monceau, eating spice
cake, succumbing to a Belgian speculoos biscuit,
going into a house with the smell of cinnamon-
flavored apples in the air . . .

. . . asking a group of three punks sporting Mohican hairstyles and Doc Martens the way one rainy winter evening at the deserted exit from the Censier-Daubenton Métro station as they fooled around in the shelter of a porch, and then being escorted by three considerate young men: "Of course we're coming with you, you wouldn't have found the way by yourself, and you might need protection at this time of night . . . ," driving at breakneck speed down the empty motorway to the west that had just been opened in a luxurious Facel-Vega lined with blond leather that smelled of honey, often adding wine to bacon soup in the country, eating rustic cheeses during the war when maggots leapt athletically out of them, their little bodies curving in the air, having stopped at Sully-sur-Loire during the exodus in 1940 to hand glasses of water with my big sister, then aged nine, to the soldiers taken prisoner who kept filing past (we were allowed to do it, adults were

not), remembering my sixteenth birthday and a
wide-skirted white dress with a pattern of large
green polka dots and a big collar, a later red faille
silk dress with a close-fitting top and a flared skirt
and two little white organdie wings at the shoul-
ders, also a short dress made of openwork black
lace, very close-fitting and with a square neck-
line, and another dress, chestnut-colored velvet
with a laced waistcoat in a golden-brown her-
ringbone fabric, a wide black leather belt form-
ing a corselet and a pair of bright purple shoes
with silver high heels for dancing; always feeling
slightly uneasy in front of the depths of one of
those large, heavy Burgundian wardrobes lined
with fabric with a dark green moiré effect, where
you feel that if you slipped into it you might be
swallowed up by the darkness or emerge into a
bright light, marveling to hear, in your head, the
voices of several people now dead but not all of
them, no, and without knowing why you hear
these voices and not others; playing with your
fingers, feeling like a stone closed in on itself, and
at moments of intense fear, discomfort, or emotion in your life knocking at a tall wooden door

with a copper knocker; closing your eyes the
better to hear the sound of the wind in tall pop-
lar trees and feeling it blow on your face; hating
hair hanging in your eyes or wearing lipstick or
having scarves tied tightly round your neck, or
a handbag carried over your elbow, or wearing
flesh-colored underclothes or anything fitting so
tightly that it cuts you under the arms; making
sure you are paid with a small coin when giving
someone a present of a knife or a letter opener;
enjoying witty remarks, a sense of humor, even
facetious comments or irony but hating sarcasm;
instinctively seeking out what is unusual, incongruous, discordant; the light of all that is strange
that passes over like lightning, but also graceful
movements, pretty gestures, a supple way of getting out of an armchair, knowing that thinking
makes time pass fast and you will emerge dis-
concerted; liking Gloria Grahame's pointed chin,
her sparkling eyes, and her cascading laughter;
fearing quicksands or a mudslide, or feeling your
foot turn over or falling flat on your back on the
tall, narrow steps of the Mexican pyramids; making lavish bunches of hydrangeas; replying with

a smile to the silent question asked by all small babies: "Who on earth are you?"

o o o

As you can see, my dear friend, we're not talking about high-flown metaphysical speculation, or profound reflections on the vanity of existence, or the passionate private life of everyone on earth. We are simply concerned with the way to make everything in life a treasure of grace and beauty that always keeps growing of its own accord, in a place where you can draw on it daily. There's no real magic in any of that, is there? In this eclectic jumble there will surely be feelings, sensations, emotions, and moments of happiness that you, too, have felt and still feel. And you have your own stock of memories which ask nothing better than to resurface, keep you company, and support you in all you have yet to do. I have learnt to recognize them for what they are: the pleasing milestones of our lives. All at once they become so much richer and more interesting than we think. And above all, tell yourself that none of all that can ever be taken away from you.

Turning the page

There's no magic about it, I wrote to the friend I'm addressing in this letter. No, but nonetheless it is of the utmost importance. Who am "I," beyond the superficial definitions that might be made of me: physical appearance, character in broad outline, relationships with other people, professional and personal connections, ties with family and friends, reputation, commitments, the networks to which I belong—beyond such definitions, which may be accurate but are also artificially constructed and deceptive, who, in a more profound sense, am I? And the "I" which is our wealth consists of opening up to the world—an aptitude for observation, an empathy with life, an ability to be at one with reality. "I" am not only a thinking, acting being, but also one with the capacity for feeling and experience, in accordance with the laws of a subterranean energy that is always being renewed. Stripped entirely of curiosity, empathy, desire, the ability to feel distress and pleasure, what would the "I" who also thinks, talks, and acts be?

I wanted to track down the imperceptible force that animates and defines us. It depends on the story of our lives, of course, but it does not hark back to the past; even if we ignore the fact, it is the quintessence and justification of all that we do now and will do in the future. "I" would not be what I am if certain events that channeled the course of my life had not occurred, or if "I" had not had the chance of feeling this or that emotion, responding to such and such an occasion, having this, that, or the other physical experience.

This book is a plea for us to recognize not simply the small, artless influence of childhood but the whole complex affective domain that forms and continues to form us, sensitive beings that we are. A plea for us not to be simply obsessed by targets—careers to be created, enterprises to be undertaken, profits to be secured—while losing sight of the "I" who entered the arena in the first place. A plea for us to understand that the profound engine of curiosity is at work in us, sustaining the ever-renewed feat of living, the benevolent and empathetic or critical and constituent view that "I" take of the world all around me.

We should give ourselves time to compile an intimate anthology of sensuality that can nonetheless be shared, a fundamental substrate of the "human condition." In using that expression and many others (think of the "vale of tears" that existence on this earth is supposed to be!), we always approach the scalding experience of pain and the crucial fact of death. Yes, but the human condition also implies the capacity for longing and desire, the ability to feel, to be moved, touched, full of emotion, and to communicate all that to others who understand this common language.

"I" am also made up of what I remember, but what rules govern our selection of memories? That selection operates without the intervention of the will, and psychoanalysis has a great deal to say about the reasons for needing to forget, although not all lost memories are due to the working of the unconscious mind. The incident itself is lost, but the essence of it remains, making its mark on the body, and that essence will reappear in response to the fleeting magic of a reminiscence, the thrill of a sensation, the surprisingly acute and sometimes incomprehensible strength of an emotion. What calls it forth if not that burning internal voice, the vital dynamo that we do not even know we have developed over the course of time? The memory itself may have gone, but the sensual memory of the body still speaks of it. We are made of material provided with sensors which record the tenacious impressions that guard and guide us. We would be paralyzed by too many memories. But the prototypes of what, in the great range of potential emotions, really touches us remain.

We are not so far from Proust here. However, the taste of a madeleine does not in itself revive a memory. That comes of sensory unrest recalling the same sensual turmoil in childhood, thanks to a ceremonial in which the essence of it all— a concentration of the confined atmosphere, the exceptional character of the incident, the time, the person of the child's aunt, the tea, the madeleine—was about to take wing, like a well-aimed arrow flying through the air, and take root forever in the sweet, slightly insipid odor of a little sponge cake, that is to say the odor of the sensations experienced at the time, which was perhaps the aspect best suited to condense the perpetual vitality of all these combined elements for the child concerned.

In a way each of us provides evidence of the sensualism elaborated by the French philosopher Condillac: The world exists through our senses before existing in more ordered fashion in our minds, and we should do all we can to preserve the creative faculty of sense throughout our lives: seeing, hearing, observing, understanding, touching, caressing, smelling, inhaling, tasting, exercising the faculty of "taste," for everyone, for others, for life itself.

Some References

Films and TV Series

Agatha Christie's Poirot, British TV series, (David Suchet).

A High Wind in Jamaica, Alexander Mackendrick, 1965.

Alien, Ridley Scott, 1979.

Ally McBeal, American TV series by David E. Kelley.

Amarcord, Federico Fellini, 1974.

Animal documentary in the series *Chroniques de l'Afrique sauvage* (Dying Cheetah).

Bad Day at Black Rock, John Sturges, 1955 (Spencer Tracy).

Dark Passage, Delmer Daves, 1947 (Agnes Moorehead).

Dune, David Lynch, 1984.

Frankenstein, James Whale, 1931.

Gone With the Wind, Victor Fleming, 1939.

House, American TV series, David Shore.

King Kong, Merian C. Cooper and Ernest B. Schoedsack, 1933.

Kiss Me Deadly, Robert Aldrich, 1955.

Kiss of Death, Henry Hathaway, 1979 (Richard Widmark).

Morse, British TV series by Colin Dexter.

My Darling Clementine, John Ford, 1946 (Henry Fonda).

NCIS (Naval Criminal Investigative Service), American TV series by Donald P. Bellisario and Don McGill.

Out of Africa, Sydney Pollack, 1985.

Peau d'âne, Jacques Demy, 1970.

Queen Kelly, Erich von Stroheim, 1928.

Taxi Driver, Martin Scorsese, 1976 (Robert De Niro).

The Age of Innocence, Martin Scorsese, 1993.

The Bear, Jean-Jacques Annaud, 1988 (Tchéky Karyo).

The Dead, John Huston, 1987.

The Ghost and Mrs. Muir, Joseph L. Mankiewicz, 1947 (Gene Tierney).

The Incredible Shrinking Man, Jack Arnold, 1957.

The Navigator, Buster Keaton and Donald Crisp, 1924 (Buster Keaton).

The Treasure of the Sierra Madre, John Huston, 1948.

The Wolf of the Malveneurs, Guillaume Radot, 1943.

What's Eating Gilbert Grape, Lasse Hallström, 1993 (Leonardo DiCaprio).

Without Apparent Motive, Philippe Labro, 1971 (Jean-Louis Trintignant).

Other References

Dorothy Baker, *Young Man with a Horn*, 1938 (Bix Beiderbecke, 1903–31).

Simone de Beauvoir, *Le deuxième sexe* (The Second Sex), 1949.

Cahiers du cinéma, journal founded in 1951 by André Bazin, Jacques Doniol-Valcroze and Joseph-Marie Lo Duca.

Jean Cocteau, *L'Aigle à deux têtes* (The Eagle with Two Heads), 1947.

Frank Herbert, *Dune*, 1965.

Patricia Highsmith, *A Dog's Ransom*, 1972.

Mary Ann Shaffer, and Annie Barrows *The Guernsey Literary and Potato Peel Pie Society*, 2009.

Pieter Jansz Saenredam, Flemish painter (1597–1665).

Franz Schubert, *Die Winterreise*, cycle of lieder.

Jean Vauthier, *La nouvelle mandragore* (The New Mandrake), after Niccoló Macchiavelli's *La mandragola*, play directed by Gérard Philipe in 1952 at the Théâtre National Populaire.

What activities offer
you the sweetness of life?

About the Author

FRANÇOISE HÉRITIER is an anthropologist and professor emerita at the Collège de France and the École des Hautes Études en Sciences Sociales. She is the author of such highly successful works as *Masculin/feminin* and *De la violence*, which has been translated into more than ten languages.